FREEDOM'S PROMISE

THE GRAND
CONTRABAND
CAMP

BY DUCHESS HARRIS, JD, PHD

Cover image: Escaped slaves sought refuge at
contraband camps in the 1860s.

Core Library

An Imprint of Abdo Publishing
abdobooks.com

abdocorelibrary.com

Printed in the United States of America, North Mankato, Minnesota
092018
012019

THIS BOOK CONTAINS RECYCLED MATERIALS

Cover Photo: National Park Service
Interior Photos: National Park Service, 1; Smith Collection/Gado/Archive Photos/Getty Images, 5; Bettmann/Getty Images, 6–7; Library of Congress, 9; National Park Service, 12–13; North Wind Picture Archives, 16–17, 20; Red Line Editorial, 18, 29; Everett Historical/Shutterstock Images, 24, 26–27; MPI/Archive Photos/Getty Images, 30, 43; William Morris Smith/Bettmann/Getty Images, 33; Astrid Riecken/The Washington Post/Getty Images, 36–37; Everett Historical/Shutterstock Images, 39

Editor: Maddie Spalding
Series Designer: Claire Vanden Branden
Contributor: Martha London

Library of Congress Control Number: 2018949705

Publisher's Cataloging-in-Publication Data

Names: Harris, Duchess, author.
Title: The grand contraband camp / by Duchess Harris.
Description: Minneapolis, Minnesota : Abdo Publishing, 2019 | Series: Freedom's promise | Includes online resources and index.
Identifiers: ISBN 9781532117695 (lib. bdg.) | ISBN 9781641856034 (pbk) | ISBN 9781532170553 (ebook)
Subjects: LCSH: United States--History--Civil War, 1861-1865--Participation, African American--Juvenile literature. | Contraband of war--Law and legislation--Juvenile literature. | Enslaved persons--Juvenile literature. | Slaves--Emancipation--Juvenile literature.
Classification: DDC 973.71--dc23

CONTENTS

A LETTER FROM DUCHESS

The word *contraband* has several meanings. It often refers to illegally traded goods. In the Civil War, it meant an enslaved person who escaped to the Union lines.

I had never heard of this term while growing up. It wasn't until recently that I learned that my grandfather's family was from the area near the Grand Contraband Camp in Fort Monroe, Virginia.

In 1861 three enslaved men were sent to help the southern war effort. They did not want to help the South and instead escaped. They sought safety at Fort Monroe, which was being run by Union general Benjamin Butler.

Before the Civil War, slaveholders could legally request the return of escaped slaves. But Virginia had rebelled against the United States. Because of this, General Butler felt he did not have to return the three men. He would hold them as "contraband of war."

I hope you enjoy this book and join me in a journey that tells the story of the promise of freedom.

Duchess Harris

Former slaves pose for a photograph in front of a Virginia farmhouse in 1862.

THE FIRST CONTRABAND CAMP

I n the spring of 1861, the United States went to war with itself. This conflict was called the American Civil War (1861–1865). The two sides involved were the Union and the Confederacy. Northern states had formed the Union. The Confederacy was made up of southern states. The Confederacy wanted to keep slavery. The Union opposed the expansion of slavery. Some people in the Union wanted to end slavery altogether.

An illustration depicts the arrival of the first escaped slaves to Fort Monroe, the site of the first contraband camp.

The state of Virginia seceded from the Union in April 1861. It joined the Confederacy. But some Union troops were still in the state after war broke out. On the outskirts of Hampton, Virginia, the Union Army was busy at Fort Monroe strengthening defenses. Fort Monroe was an important Union base against the Confederate Army.

On the evening of May 23, 1861, three black men got in a boat. They rowed across Hampton Roads Harbor to Fort Monroe. The men's names were Shepard Mallory, James Townsend, and Frank Baker. They were fleeing a Confederate base near Norfolk, Virginia. Norfolk was on the opposite side of the harbor from Fort Monroe. The men's slaveholder was a Confederate colonel. He had sent them to the Confederate base to help build weapons for the Confederate Army.

The men had learned that their slaveholder planned to send them to North Carolina. If this happened, the men would be far away from their families. Their families

Benjamin Butler was a politician and a Union general during the Civil War.

were enslaved with them in Virginia. The men had a decision to make. If they stayed with their slaveholder, they might never see their families again. If they tried to seek refuge at Fort Monroe, there wasn't any guarantee of their safety. The soldiers at Fort Monroe might turn them away or shoot at them. But there was a chance that the Union soldiers would allow them to stay at the fort. Then the men may never be enslaved again. So they had decided to escape.

The men soon arrived at the fort. General Benjamin Butler met with them. Butler was the fort's commanding officer. The men told him about being forced to work for the Confederacy. They were hoping for safety behind Union lines.

Butler considered what to do. The United States had passed the Fugitive Slave Act in 1850. This law said that he needed to return these men to their slaveholder. But Butler did not want to do this. Their slaveholder had forced them to make weapons. These weapons were helping the Confederate Army fight the Union Army. Butler knew the men would be forced to continue to help the Confederate cause if he returned them. So he tried to think of a way around the Fugitive Slave Act.

While Butler thought about what to do, the men stayed in the fort. They waited to learn their fate. If they were turned away now, their slaveholder would punish them severely.

THE SOLUTION

Butler found a loophole in the Fugitive Slave Act. Slaves were considered property. Butler used this idea to his advantage. He called the men "war contraband." Contraband is enemy property that helps the war effort. The Union Army could legally take away Confederate contraband. Under this reasoning, the Union Army allowed the men to stay in the fort.

News of Butler's decision spread. Hundreds of enslaved people fled to Fort Monroe. They began to live in the abandoned nearby town of Hampton. Similar camps were established in other parts of the South. They were also built near Union-held lands. These camps were called

A painting shows what Fort Monroe looked like in the 1860s.

contraband camps. The camp near Fort Monroe became known as the Grand Contraband Camp.

CONTRABAND CAMPS

Contraband camps got their name from the people who lived in them. Enslaved people who escaped from their slaveholders were still seen as property. Even though

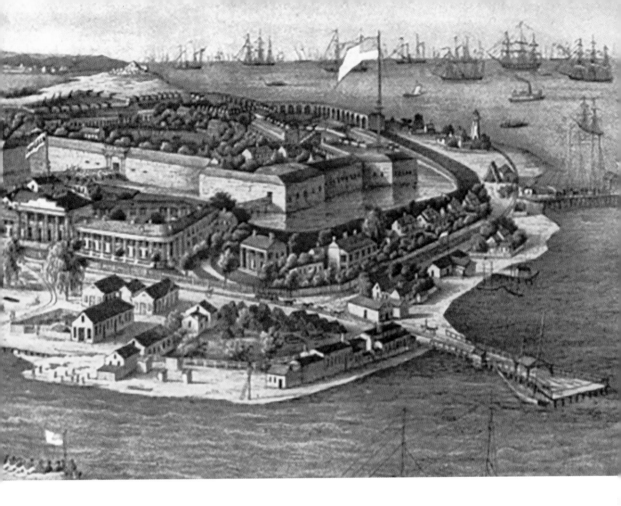

they were safe behind Union lines, they were not
considered free. The law said they were possessions,
not people.

In August 1861, Congress passed the first
Confiscation Act. This act allowed the Union Army
to take enslaved people living in the Confederacy.

STUDYING THE CAMP

Archaeologists today continue to study the Grand Contraband Camp. They started exploring a small section of Hampton in 2014 to learn more about the people who lived there. The soil gave the archaeologists the most useful information. The color of the soil indicated where a garbage pile, a cellar, or a fence line had been built. Archaeologists found that the buildings had been built close together. One of the artifacts they found was a Union Navy button. This suggests that black residents fought aboard Union ships in the navy.

The Union Army was allowed to do this because the Confederacy was in rebellion against the United States. Taking away enslaved people from the Confederacy weakened its labor force.

People who lived in contraband camps were considered contraband only in name. Contraband camps allowed formerly enslaved people to live as if they were free. They could marry legally for the first time. Large contraband camps operated more like towns than camps. These camps were largely independent from the Union Army. Army forts often did not have a lot of extra supplies to share. So camp residents built their own shops. They made and sold food. They started their own schools and churches.

Many contraband camp residents worked for the Union Army. Over the course of the Civil War, many of these people enlisted with the Union to fight for their freedom. They helped change the course of the Civil War.

EXPLORE ONLINE

Chapter One discusses the creation of contraband camps. Visit the website below for more information on this topic. How is the information from the website the same as the information in Chapter One? What new information did you learn from the website?

THE CONTRABAND OF AMERICA AND THE ROAD TO FREEDOM
abdocorelibrary.com/grand-contraband-camp

SLAVERY AND THE CIVIL WAR

In the mid-1800s, slavery only existed in certain parts of the United States. Vermont was the first territory to end slavery. Slavery was abolished in Vermont in 1777. Northern states mostly outlawed slavery by the early 1800s. But southern states allowed slavery.

The country did not know what to do about slavery. Some states wanted to end slavery. Others wanted to keep it. They relied on slavery for farming. The federal government decided to use a boundary line that had been created in the 1760s to divide free states from slave states. This boundary line was called the Mason-Dixon Line. Most of the states that were

Enslaved people did hard labor, such as picking cotton, in the South.

SLAVERY IN THE UNITED STATES

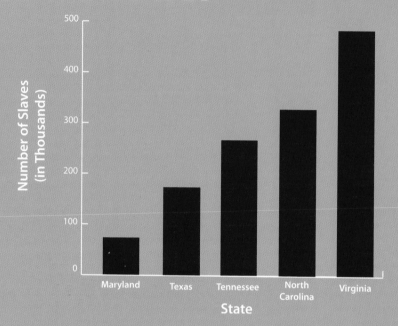

Before the Civil War began, nearly 4 million people were enslaved in the United States. The above graph shows how many people were enslaved in certain US states in 1860. How does this graph help you understand where slavery was common in the United States at the time?

north of the line did not allow slavery. The states that were south of the line allowed slavery.

TURNER'S REBELLION

In 1831 an enslaved black man named Nat Turner led a rebellion against his slaveholder. He was enslaved on a plantation in Southampton County, Virginia. In his childhood, he had learned how to read and write. He was sold three times. He eventually became a preacher. He believed he was called by God to help free enslaved people.

On August 21, 1831, Turner and six other enslaved men killed the family of Turner's slaveholder. Then they encouraged approximately 70 other enslaved people to rebel against their slaveholders. In two days, the men killed approximately 60 white people. Most of the men were captured. But Turner escaped. He hid for about two months. After he was captured, he was tried and hanged for his crime.

Turner's rebellion caused many white people to become afraid of enslaved people. They blamed Turner's rebellion on his ability to read and write. Stricter laws were put into place. The laws forbade the education of enslaved people. Turner's rebellion also strengthened white southerners' views that slavery should not be abolished.

SLAVERY LAWS

In addition to laws that restricted enslaved people's rights, laws were later passed that made it more difficult for enslaved people to escape. The US Congress passed the Fugitive Slave Act in 1850. This act said that enslaved people who were caught trying to escape must be returned to their slaveholders. Anyone who aided a slave's escape could be punished with a fine or jail time. Southern states were threatening to secede from the Union. The Fugitive Slave Act was created to satisfy southern states and keep them from seceding.

In states that allowed slavery, there were few options for enslaved people to gain freedom. Some slaveholders allowed enslaved people to buy their freedom. But buying freedom was often expensive. The price black people were forced to pay for their freedom would equal tens of thousands of dollars today.

Enslaved people who tried to escape faced many dangers.

Sometimes enslaved people were granted freedom after the death of a slaveholder. But this was rare. Enslaved people were often sold to another family after a slaveholder's death. Some were given to the slaveholder's children or grandchildren. For many enslaved people, escape was the only way to gain freedom.

WAR AND FREEDOM

Disagreements between the northern

and southern states led to the Civil War. Abraham Lincoln was the US president during the Civil War. Lincoln initially did not call for slavery to be banned. When the Civil War began, Lincoln's only goal was to keep the United States together.

Lincoln was forced to reconsider the issue of slavery after Butler's decision at Fort Monroe. Every day when Lincoln went to work, he passed a contraband camp in Washington, DC. It soon became clear to him that the Union could not win the war without the help of black Americans.

BLEEDING KANSAS

In the mid-1800s, Kansas and Nebraska were not states yet. They were territories. Congress passed the Kansas-Nebraska Act in 1854. This act allowed the people living in the territories to decide for themselves if they wanted the territories to keep or abolish slavery. But there were many people on both sides of the argument. Neither side would give up its position. Disagreements erupted into violence. Because of this widespread violence, the Kansas territory became known as "Bleeding Kansas."

A few months after Butler's decision, Lincoln signed the first Confiscation Act. He then signed a second Confiscation Act in July 1862. This act said that enslaved people who reached Union lines would be freed.

FURTHER EVIDENCE

Chapter Two discusses slavery in the United States. What was one of the main points of this chapter? What evidence is included to support this point? Read the article at the website below. Does the information on the website support this point? Or does it present new evidence?

SLAVERY IN AMERICA
abdocorelibrary.com/grand-contraband-camp

Abraham Lincoln was president of the United States from 1861 to 1865.

LIFE IN CONTRABAND CAMPS

In 1861 many escaped slaves fled to Fort Monroe. They came from all over the country. The fort soon became crowded. The refugees eventually settled in Hampton. Hampton was an abandoned town. The Confederate Army had not wanted the Union Army to use the town or any resources in the town. So Confederate troops had burned the town to the ground in August 1861.

Escaped slaves established other contraband camps across the South. The camps took root where there was

Many escaped slaves came to Fort Monroe in the summer of 1861.

Union control. But the Union Army was often on the move. As battles were won and lost, the Union gained and lost ground. Contraband camps moved to follow the Union troops. Refugees needed the Union Army to protect them to ensure they would not be recaptured.

Refugees built homes and stores out of whatever they could find. For many people, this was their first chance at owning a home. Some camps held more than 8,000 refugees. Many of these camps looked similar to the Grand Contraband Camp.

FORT MONROE

Dutch settlers brought a group of enslaved Africans to the Virginia colony in the 1600s. This was one of the first groups of enslaved people to be brought to North America. Where the settlers landed was not far from where Fort Monroe now stands. Many people see significance in this. They see Fort Monroe as both the beginning and end of slavery in the United States.

CAMP POPULATIONS

Camp	Location	Population
Corinth Contraband Camp	Corinth, Mississippi	6,000
Grand Contraband Camp	Hampton, Virginia	9,000
New Bern Contraband Camp	New Bern, North Carolina	8,600
Murfreesboro Contraband Camp	Murfreesboro, Tennessee	2,000

The above chart shows the locations and estimated populations of some of the largest contraband camps (at their peak populations). How do you think their populations changed over time? What do you think life in these camps might have been like?

SURVIVAL IN THE CAMPS

People who came to contraband camps sometimes traveled great distances. Most of them did not have many possessions. Many just had the clothes on their backs. They were often malnourished. They had not been able to eat much food while traveling. Many slaveholders did not give enslaved people enough

Escaped slaves often did not have many belongings when they arrived at contraband camps.

to eat. When refugees arrived in the camps, the first thing they often needed was food.

Finding food in the camps was sometimes difficult. Union troops gave out some food to the camp residents, but it was low in nutritional value. It was also bland. Often the only food the troops could spare was porridge. During food shortages, the contraband camp residents were the last to be fed. Even when enough food was available, Union officials sometimes cut residents' rations. They said they did this for the residents' own good. Residents were told the lack of food would build self-reliance.

Conditions in camps varied. Some Union officers wanted to help refugees. Others did not. But even the people who wanted to help sometimes could not. They did not have the funds to buy clothes or food for the refugees. Doctors were in short supply. Aid organizations helped supply resources to camp residents. These organizations were often associated with religious groups. Churches sent volunteers to the camps. The volunteers brought food and clothing for the residents. Sometimes they brought medicine. But often this help was not enough. Diseases such as smallpox spread through the camps. Residents slept on the ground in tents. In winter, there were sometimes not enough blankets available for all of a camp's residents. One Union commander reported that in a camp in

Tennessee, nearly 30 residents died each day from cold or disease.

BLACK SOLDIERS

At the start of the Civil War, few black soldiers fought in the Union Army. Many black people wanted to fight for the army. But they were not allowed to enlist. Some were told that this was not their war. Many black Americans vowed that they would enlist with the Union Army before the war was over. They wanted to be a part of the fight for their freedom.

A group of black Union soldiers stands inside Fort Lincoln in Washington, DC.

In 1862 black Americans were allowed to enlist in the Union Army. But they were not treated the same as white soldiers. Black soldiers were paid only $7 per month. White soldiers were paid $13 per month. Black soldiers had to fight in separate units from white soldiers. Still, by the end of the Civil War, black soldiers made up nearly 10 percent of the Union Army.

African Americans also fought for the Confederacy. Toward the end of the Civil War, the Union gained ground in the southern territories. The Confederate Army was desperate. Some enslaved black people had already been supporting the Confederacy as cooks and laborers. The Confederate Army decided to allow enslaved people to enlist. Some slaveholders promised to free enslaved people who fought for the Confederacy.

SUPPORTING THE UNION

More than 475,000 contraband camp residents worked for the Union Army. Some built Union forts. Others cared for Union soldiers in hospitals. Residents also washed soldiers' clothes and cooked their meals. They took care of animals for the Union Army. The law said that contraband camp residents were supposed to be paid for this work. But the Union Army did not pay many of them. Still, camp residents saw hope in working with the Union Army. They believed that after the war ended, they would become free.

STRAIGHT TO THE
SOURCE

In 1864 escaped slave Joseph Miller and his family lived in the Camp Nelson contraband camp in Kentucky. Miller enlisted in the Union Army. But Union troops later forced his family to leave the camp. Miller wrote about this experience:

> A mounted guard came to my tent and ordered my wife and children out of Camp. . . . [The guard] told my wife and family that if they did not get up into the wagon which he had he would shoot the last one of them. On being thus threatened my wife and children went into the wagon. My wife carried her sick child in her arms. . . . I [later] found my wife and children shivering [in a house] with cold and famished with hunger. They had not received a morsel of food during the whole day. My boy was dead.

> Source: Joseph Miller. "Family and Freedom: Black Families in the American Civil War." *Freedmen and Southern Society Project.* University of Maryland, January 1987. Web. Accessed July 27, 2018.

What's the Big Idea?

Take a close look at this passage. This chapter talks about life and survival in contraband camps. How does Miller's experience compare with what you learned in this chapter?

LEGACY OF
THE CAMPS

Lincoln signed the Emancipation Proclamation on January 1, 1863. This document freed enslaved people in Union-occupied southern territories. But it did not end slavery in the slaveholding border states that fought for the Union.

The Union won the Civil War in 1865. Then the Thirteenth Amendment was passed. This amendment ended slavery. It freed the remaining enslaved people.

The Grand Contraband Camp was the first of many contraband camps. By 1865 more than 100 contraband camps had been established.

Roses sit on a memorial to freed slaves in Alexandria, Virginia.

Nearly half a million refugees lived in these contraband camps. Approximately 9,000 people lived in the Grand Contraband Camp by the end of the Civil War. The federal government sold land inside the camp to the freed slaves. They helped rebuild Hampton. Today, the city's population is still mostly African American.

African Americans formed their own schools in contraband camps. Today, Hampton University exists on the site where a woman named Mary

PERSPECTIVES

ARLINGTON NATIONAL CEMETERY

Approximately 179,000 black Americans fought in the Union Army. White soldiers who died were buried at Arlington National Cemetery in Virginia. But black soldiers who died were not buried in this cemetery. Some black soldiers wrote a letter asking for the graves of black soldiers to be moved to the cemetery. They said, "We are not contrabands, but soldiers of the U.S. Army. We . . . should share the same privileges and rights of burial in every way with our fellow soldiers, who only differ from us in color." The army did eventually move the graves to Arlington National Cemetery.

Hampton University taught many African American students in the late 1800s.

Smith Peake taught Grand Contraband Camp residents how to read and write. Hampton University was founded in 1868. It is a historically black college. A historically black college is a college that accepted black people at a time when many other schools refused to do so.

Some researchers believe the contraband movement was the first mass black rebellion in the United States. This movement of enslaved black people to Union forts paved the way for later civil

HAMPTON UNIVERSITY

Mary Smith Peake was a teacher at the Grand Contraband Camp. She was born in Norfolk, Virginia. Before arriving at the camp, she had taught free and enslaved black people how to read and write in secret in her home. At the camp, Peake taught classes underneath an oak tree. That oak tree continues to stand on the campus of Hampton University. Today the tree is called the Emancipation Oak.

rights movements. Contraband camp residents worked hard for their freedom. Their work inspired black activists in the mid-1900s. These activists fought to secure equal rights.

The Grand Contraband Camp was a symbol of hope for enslaved people. It inspired the creation of other contraband camps. Camp residents shaped the South after the Civil War. Formerly enslaved people settled throughout the country. They established black communities. In these ways, the legacy of the contraband camps lives on today.

STRAIGHT TO THE
SOURCE

William B. Gould IV is a professor at Stanford
University. Gould's great-grandfather escaped
slavery and joined the Union Army. He kept a diary
of his experiences. Professor Gould published the diary
in 2002. In an interview, he explained why he shared his
great-grandfather's story:

> This book highlights for the first time that there were a number
> of African Americans who were literate and who corresponded
> with one another. Despite the bar on literacy [for slaves] in the
> Confederate states, [my great-grandfather] had a vast network
> of correspondents. . . . My hope is that young people who are
> disadvantaged . . . will be inspired by this man.

Source: Lisa Trei. "Diary of Professor's Great-Grandfather
Helps Document Network of Literate Slaves." *Stanford
Report*. Stanford University, April 9, 2003. Web. Accessed
August 8, 2018.

Back It Up

The author of this passage is using evidence to support
a point. Write a paragraph describing the point the
author is making. Then write down two or three
pieces of evidence the author uses to make
the point.

FAST FACTS

- James Townsend, Frank Baker, and Shepard Mallory arrived at Fort Monroe in Virginia in May 1861. These black men were fleeing slavery. They sought refuge at the Union fort.

- The Fugitive Slave Act required people to return slaves to their slaveholders. But Union general Benjamin Butler found a loophole that allowed escaped black refugees to seek shelter behind Union Army lines. Enslaved people were considered property. Butler called them contraband, or enemy property that can legally be seized in times of war.

- Many enslaved people escaped to Fort Monroe. They settled in the nearby town of Hampton. Their settlement became the first contraband camp. It was called the Grand Contraband Camp.

- Contraband camps helped change the course of the Civil War. Many camp residents worked for the Union Army.

- Today, Hampton University stands on the site of the former Grand Contraband Camp.

STOP AND
THINK

You Are There

This book talks about life and survival in the contraband camps. Imagine you lived in a contraband camp in the 1860s. Write a letter home telling your friends about your experience. Be sure to add plenty of details to your letter.

Surprise Me

Chapter Two talks about the history of slavery in the United States. After reading this book, what two or three facts about slavery did you find most surprising? Write a few sentences about each fact. Why did you find each fact surprising?

Take a Stand

Abraham Lincoln signed the Emancipation Proclamation two years after Butler's decision at Fort Monroe. Do you think Lincoln could have done more to abolish slavery sooner? Why or why not?

GLOSSARY

abolish
to end something

abolitionist
someone who is
against slavery

confiscation
the process of taking
something away

emancipation
the act of freeing
enslaved people

fugitive
someone who has escaped
or is hiding from the law

malnourished
underfed
and underweight

plantation
a large area of land where
crops are grown

rations
daily supplies of food and
other resources that are
often distributed by armies
or governments

refugee
someone who is looking
for safety

secede
to separate from
the whole

ONLINE RESOURCES

To learn more about the Grand Contraband Camp, visit our free resource websites below.

Visit **abdocorelibrary.com** for free Common Core resources for teachers and students, including vetted activities, multimedia, and booklinks, for deeper subject comprehension.

Visit **abdobooklinks.com** for free additional online weblinks for further learning. These links are routinely monitored and updated to provide the most current information available.

LEARN MORE

Halls, Kelly Milner. *Life during the Civil War*. Minneapolis, MN: Abdo Publishing, 2015.

Rissman, Rebecca. *Slavery in the United States*. Minneapolis, MN: Abdo Publishing, 2015.

ABOUT THE AUTHOR

Duchess Harris, JD, PhD
Professor Harris is the chair of the American Studies department at Macalester College and curator of the Duchess Harris Collection of ABDO books. She is the author and coauthor of recently released ABDO books including *Hidden Human Computers: The Black Women of NASA*, *Black Lives Matter*, and *Race and Policing*.

Before working with ABDO, she authored several other books on the topics of race, culture, and American history. She served as an associate editor for *Litigation News*, the American Bar Association Section of Litigation's quarterly flagship publication, and was the first editor in chief of *Law Raza*, an interactive online journal covering race and the law, published at William Mitchell College of Law. She has earned a PhD in American Studies from the University of Minnesota and a JD from William Mitchell College of Law.

INDEX